Good Granny / Bad Granny

Good Granny / Bad Granny

By Mary McHugh

Illustrations by Patrice Storms

CHRONICLE BOOKS

Text copyright © 2007 by Mary McHugh.
Illustrations copyright © 2007 by Patricia Storms.

Library of Congress Cataloging-in-Publication Data:

McHugh, Mary.
  Good Granny/Bad Granny / by Mary McHugh.
    p. cm.
  ISBN-13: 978-0-8118-5592-1
  ISBN-10: 0-8118-5592-9
1. Grandmothers—Humor. 2. Grandparenting—Humor. I. Title.

  PN6231.G8M34 2007
  306.874'50207—dc22

                    2006026390

Manufactured in China

Designed by Ayako Akazawa

Distributed in Canada by Raincoast Books
9050 Shaughnessy Street
Vancouver, British Columbia V6P 6E5

10 9 8 7 6 5 4 3 2 1

Chronicle Books LLC
680 Second Street
San Francisco, California 94107

www.chroniclebooks.com

All you grandmothers out there know

that having grandchildren is one of life's great experiences. Sure, you had to wait patiently until your children turned 33 before they grudgingly got married. Then you had to keep your mouth shut for five years before they found the time to fit having a child into their busy schedules. Now, *finally*, there's this beautiful baby in your life. And what makes the baby even more beautiful is that you didn't have to go through nine more months of bloating and weight gain and feeling really fat and struggling to get out of chairs. None of that. This new little being came into your life without any contractions or mind-numbing pain. No mess, no struggle, no pushing. Just the sight of your daughter or daughter-in-law holding an exquisite infant with a cherub's mouth and the eyes of an angel. All that's expected of you is that you exclaim, "Oh, what a beautiful child!"

You aren't responsible for the way this one turns out. You can go home whenever you want to. You don't have to feel guilty for anything you do. You only have to love your grandchild. And that's the easiest thing you've done since conceiving your own children. No child is more perfect than your grandchild. As the baby starts turning into a person who laughs when he sees you, reaches out to you to be picked up, grabs your nose with his little hand, then crawls, walks, and learns to say "Nanny" or "Granny" or anything he wants, you are totally bewitched, completely in love. There is no other experience in life quite like being a grandmather.

Then comes the dilemma. Should you be a good grandmother and do all the things you are supposed to do—all the things you know your children want and expect you to do? In other words, do you have to be an old-fashioned, well-behaved grandmother? You know—the kind who cooks only healthful, nutritious meals; makes sure this child has rich cultural experiences and educational toys; behaves in a dignified manner at all times; and is available at any hour of the day or night to babysit? Or should you be a bad grandmother and do whatever you know the child would love—things parents would never let him do: trips to the racetrack, raids on Kentucky Fried Chicken, and videogame marathons? And how about doing something *you* want to do once in a while, instead of what your grandchild wants to do: cruising in the Caribbean instead of going to a bar mitzvah, or going to your yoga class instead of babysitting.

You're torn. Good Granny. Bad Granny. It's too hard to decide, so on one page, you'll find all the things good grannies do, and on the other, you'll find out what bad grannies (read: fun grannies) do.

We'll never tell anyone which one you choose. Follow your heart, and if you'd rather take a child to Atlantic City than to the science museum, go for it. If you've always secretly wanted to teach a child to make mud pies instead of baking chocolate chip cookies, put on old clothes and do it. It's up to you.

You'll find lots of ideas that will delight your grandchildren —and maybe even their parents. They're grandparents-in-training, after all. But whatever you do, have fun and enjoy those children before they turn into annoying adults. You only have a short time to bend these children in your direction, so get to work. Spoil them, delight them, shock them, teach them, and unleash some interesting people into the world.

Good Granny tucks her grandchildren into bed at 8 p.m. and reads them *Goodnight Moon*.

Bad Granny lets them stay up to watch David Letterman and feeds them Cracker Jacks.

Good Granny takes her grandchildren to Disney World and lets them hug Mickey Mouse.

Bad Granny takes them to Las Vegas and teaches them to play the slots.

Good Granny prepares nourishing lunches of salads and whole wheat bread.

Bad Granny orders fried chicken by the bucket, with a side order of fries.

Good Granny buys her grandchildren
LEGO sets for their birthdays.

Bad Granny buys them wicked-sounding guns and evil-looking swords.

Good Granny takes her grandchildren to the movies to see *Bambi*.

Bad Granny sneaks them in to see
Invasion of the Body Snatchers.

Good Granny takes her grandchildren
to baseball games and does
the wave with them.

Bad Granny takes them to World Wrestling Entertainment matches.

Good Granny takes her grandchildren to petting zoos.

Bad Granny takes them to
the racetrack and teaches them how
to handicap the horses.

Good Granny loves to ride on merry-go-rounds with her grandchildren.

Bad Granny takes them to the scariest ride of them all: Space Mountain at Disney World.

Good Granny takes her grandchildren to the mall to shop for educational toys.

Bad Granny takes them to the mall and teaches them to max out their parents' credit cards.

Good Granny buys her granddaughters
Laura Ashley dresses.

Bad Granny buys them tank tops and really low-cut jeans.

Good Granny takes her grandchildren
ice-skating and makes them hot chocolate
with marshmallows.

Bad Granny takes her grandchildren to hockey games and gives them super-size sodas.

Good Granny teaches her grandchildren to make roast chicken and baked potatoes, with gingerbread cookies for dessert.

Bad Granny shows them how to look up take-out restaurants in the Yellow Pages.

Good Granny keeps a supply of markers, finger paints, and crayons to encourage her grandchildren to be creative.

Bad Granny keeps Spider-Man comic books around for her grandchildren to read, so they will keep quiet while she watches her soap operas.

Good Granny settles fights among her grandchildren by telling them they should love their brothers and sisters.

Bad Granny tells her grandchildren, "Go ahead and torture each other. It's good training for the real world."

Good Granny teaches her grandchildren how to knit.

Bad Granny shows them how to download rap music onto their iPods.

Good Granny teaches her grandchildren to grow beautiful roses that climb over the garden gate.

Bad Granny teaches her grandchildren to buy a dozen roses at the supermarket for $14.99.

Good Granny is still married to her original husband.

Bad Granny is in the Bahamas marrying step-granddaddy No. 3.

Good Granny wears tasteful shirtdresses and sensible shoes.

Bad Granny borrows her granddaughter's micro-mini and platform heels.

Good Granny wears a little bit of lipstick when she takes her grandchildren out and tells everyone she's their grandmother.

Bad Granny buys every new blush, eye shadow, lip gloss, and age-defying moisturizer she can find, and when she's with her grandchildren, she says, "Everyone thinks I'm their mother."

Good Granny plays Chutes and Ladders
with her grandchildren any time
they ask her to.

Bad Granny hogs the controls
of their Xbox.

Good Granny takes her grandchildren to the science museum and walks them through the giant model of the beating heart.

Bad Granny takes her grandchildren to the car museum at Daytona Beach and drives them around the track at 180 miles per hour.

Good Granny takes her grandchildren to the planetarium and shows them the constellation of Orion in the skies.

Bad Granny reads them their horoscopes
and tells them every word is true.

Good Granny never visits without calling first.

Bad Granny pops in unannounced at ten o'clock in the morning with paintball guns and a gallon of ice cream.

Good Granny scrubs everything in sight
and puts away all breakables before her
grandchildren come to visit.

Bad Granny leaves everything in her house the way it is and takes her grandchildren out for lunch at fast food.

Good Granny has no desire whatsoever to appear on TV. She'd much rather stay home and play with her grandchildren.

Bad Granny goes on *American Idol* and embarrasses her grandchildren by dedicating her song to them before singing "My Way."

Good Granny knits warm socks and mittens for her grandchildren.

Bad Granny takes her grandchildren to Neiman Marcus and buys them fingerless gloves and motorcycle boots.

Good Granny takes her grandchildren to the county fair and buys them fruit pies.

Bad Granny takes her grandchildren to the county fair and stuffs them with elephant ears, funnel cakes, and cotton candy, then rides the roller coaster with them.

Good Granny never misses a christening, confirmation, bar mitzvah, graduation, or wedding of her grandchildren.

Bad Granny is always on a cruise whenever a grandchild is christened, confirmed, bar mitzvahed, graduated, or wed, but she sends big checks to make up for it.

Good Granny only has an occasional glass of Chardonnay because she wants to set a good example for her grandchildren.

Bad Granny drinks really good wine at dinner every night, then tells her grandchildren drinking is bad for them.

Good Granny lets a crying grandchild sleep in her bed when there's a thunderstorm.

Bad Granny makes popcorn during a thunderstorm and puts on a DVD of *The Godfather* to take her grandchildren's minds off the storm.

Good Granny lets her grandchildren play in a bubble bath every night.

Bad Granny lets them run under the lawn
sprinkler instead of making them take a bath.

Good Granny keeps a camera nearby when she's with her grandchildren and photographs them whenever they do *anything*.

Bad Granny hands her camera to a grandchild and says, "Take a picture of me —I just had my hair highlighted."

Good Granny never uses the word "no"
when she's with her grandchildren.

Bad Granny says "no" all the time: "No, you don't have to eat that broccoli if you hate it—leave it for the waiter." "No, you don't have to have a bath tonight if you don't want to. We'll go swimming tomorrow."

Good Granny goes bike riding with her grandchildren in the park near her house.

Bad Granny roars off into the sunset with her grandchildren on the back of her Harley.

Good Granny plays Go Fish with her grandchildren over and over and over again, and loves it.

Bad Granny teaches her grandchildren to play Texas Hold 'Em for money and says, "You get way too much allowance anyway."

Good Granny plays Monopoly with her grandchildren and sells them Park Place if they already have Broadway.

Bad Granny plays Monopoly with her grandchildren and tells them Baltic Avenue is a good property to buy.

Good Granny plays basketball with her grandchildren and misses every time she tries for a basket.

Bad Granny doesn't tell her grandchildren she was star center on her high school basketball team and hustles them for a quarter a game.

Good Granny takes her grandchildren on nature walks and points out every robin, squirrel, and oak tree along the way.

Bad Granny takes her grandchildren for walks in the city and points out every outlet store having a sale and every restaurant with a *prix fixe* under $20.

Good Granny tells her 10-year-old granddaughter she's beautiful just the way God made her.

Bad Granny takes her granddaughter to
the most exclusive hair stylist she can find
and makes her *feel* beautiful.

When **Good Granny** babysits, she says to her daughter or daughter-in-law, "Just run along and have a good time, dear. You don't have to get back early for me."

When *Bad Granny* babysits, she says to her daughter or daughter-in-law, "Have a good time, honey, but be sure to be back in time for my yoga class."

Good Granny understands that her grandchildren won't have much to say to her from the ages of 14 to 18, and she accepts it.

Bad Granny buys her uncommunicative teenaged grandchildren iPods so they have an excuse not to talk to her.

Good Granny doesn't own a cell phone, and still calls her grandchildren on their house phones and wonders why they never return her calls.

Bad Granny never turns her cell phone off, and calls her grandchildren from the beauty salon just to check up on them.

Good Granny thanks God every day
for giving her grandchildren
she can take care of.

Bad Granny thanks God every day
for giving her grandchildren
she can have fun with.